W0187682

ABOVE, BELOW AND LONG AGO

Michael Bright and
Jonathan Emmerson

WAYLAND

N NATURAL
HISTORY
MUSEUM

First published in Great Britain in 2022
by Wayland

Text copyright © Hodder and Stoughton, 2022
Illustrations copyright © Jonathan Emmerson, 2022

All rights reserved

Editor: Sarah Peutrill
Designer: Peter Scoulding

ISBN: 978 1 5263 1812 1 (HB)
ISBN: 978 1 5263 1813 8 (PB)
ISBN: 978 1 5263 2470 2 (EBook)

Printed and bound in Dubai

Wayland, an imprint of
Hachette Children's Group
Part of Hodder and Stoughton
Carmelite House
50 Victoria Embankment
London EC4Y 0DZ

An Hachette UK Company
www.hachette.co.uk
www.hachettechildrens.co.uk

FSC
www.fsc.org

MIX
Paper from
responsible sources
FSC® C104740

Contents

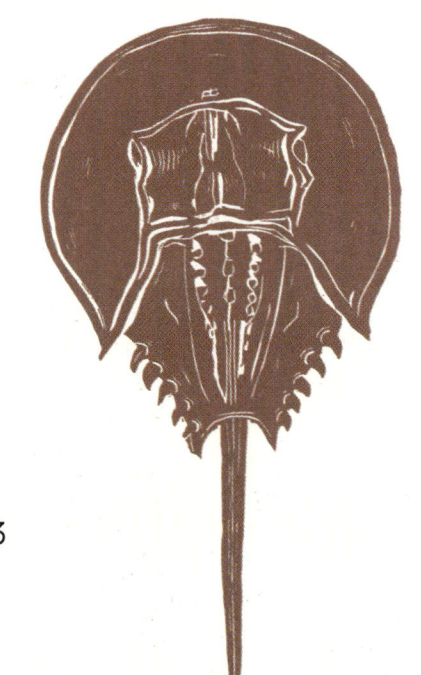

Hard to See

*Wildlife can be quite hard to see
sometimes, unless you know when
and where to look.*

There are plants and animals that live in difficult-to-get-at
places, such as cliffs and mountains or caves and
burrows below the ground. Some come out only at night when
we're all asleep. Others simply disappear for part of the year,
when they move to places where the weather and supply of food
is better, or vanish in front of our eyes by blending in with their
background. There are a few that, during the course of their lives,
change from one form to another, like the elver that becomes an
eel. Others died long ago and, over the course of millions of years,
simply turned to stone and became fossils. At one time,
people thought all this was magic!

Above

Plants and animals on cliffs and mountains are really hard to find, unless you are a very good rock climber. You might glimpse a bird in flight, but some fly so fast that you'll only see them for a few moments.

LIFE IN THE SKY

Birds fly across the world, soaring high above the seas and the continents. They fly long distances to be in the best places to feed, nest and bring up their young.

Bar-headed geese have a slightly larger wing area than other geese, so they can fly in thin air, such as when travelling in V-formation over Mount Everest. It's the world's highest bird migration.

CLIFFSIDE LIFE

Cliffs are safe places for birds to nest as land predators cannot reach them; and on high ground are plants and animals that are so adapted to cliffside life that they even invade man-made 'cliffs' in cities.

MOUNTAIN LIFE

Higher up on mountain slopes, plants and animals must endure harsh conditions, but up there in the thin air, where breathing is difficult, are some very special mountaineers.

Atlantic Puffin

The Atlantic puffin is a multitasking bird. It not only flies, but also swims and tunnels. In spring, it digs a burrow for its nest on the tops of sheer cliffs on remote islands, safe from predators such as foxes. But spring is the only time that you might see this bird, because most of its life is spent in the open ocean, hunting fish by diving and swimming underwater.

WEATHER FORECASTER

The puffin's brightly coloured bill during the breeding season has earned it the nickname 'clown of the air', but it is far from a joke. Icelandic folklore suggests that puffins can predict the weather, and there is some truth in it. Local fishermen watch their behaviour. If they return to the nest site and choose not to go back to sea, it's a sure sign there's a storm brewing.

Snow Leopard

The snow leopard lives in high mountains, from eastern Afghanistan to western China, though the chances of ever seeing one are very small. Its light-coloured, black-spotted fur blends in with the rocky and snowy background, and, as long as the cat keeps still, it's almost invisible.

INVISIBLE MOUNTAIN CAT

Scientists must trek into the remote mountain areas and then sit and wait patiently for many hours, or even days, before one appears. Only when the snow leopard moves do they have a chance of seeing it.

HUNTER AND HUNTED

Snow leopards are on the move when hunting mountain goats and sheep, such as the markhor, Himalayan tahr and Himalayan blue sheep. The leopards leap from one narrow ledge to the next on sheer cliff faces, using their long bushy tail to help them balance. Their beautiful fur, though, means that humans hunt them, which also means that snow leopards are becoming increasingly rare.

Spanish Mountain Flower

There is a little plant, with heart-shaped leaves and tiny green flowers, which grows in cracks in a particular limestone cliff on the Spanish side of the Pyrenees. It is found nowhere else in the world.

SHEER CLIFFS

The plant is almost impossible to see, as the knife-like crags are almost vertical, but it can grow in this dry and out-of-the-way place because of ants. The ants pollinate the flowers and carry away the seeds; so, new seedlings often grow out of ants' nests.

VERY SPECIAL PLANT

The plant grows very slowly and may live for 300 years, but it depends almost entirely on the ants. If they should abandon the cliff face, the plant could become extinct. The species has survived for millions of years, from a time when the world was much warmer, and so is known as a 'relict species'. It has no English common name, but it is related to the yam, and scientists call it *Borderea chouardii*. It is one of the rarest and slowest-growing plants in the world.

Rocky Mountain Goat

The mountain goat is built for a life in the Rocky Mountains of North America.

CLIFF CLIMBERS

It has a thick undercoat and an outer layer of long, hollow hairs that keep the animal warm in winter. Its powerful neck and shoulder muscles help it climb steep slopes. Its feet are adapted to clamber along the narrowest rocky ledges. The inner pads on the soles of its feet are like climbing shoes that give it grip, and its cloven hooves spread apart and ensure it has good footing and balance on the slippery slopes.

FIGHTING GOATS

The goats are often seen clambering about on sheer cliffs at dizzying heights, and they do fall occasionally, especially when fighting. They do a lot of fighting. Males fight in the breeding season, but females are even more aggressive. They fight all year round, sometimes four or five times in an hour. The reason is that cliffside ledges do not accommodate crowds, and so fights ensure groups of goats do not join together, but remain small and separate.

Leaf-eared Mouse

At the top of Llullaillaco volcano in the Andes Mountains of South America, there lives a far from ordinary mouse.

MIGHTY MOUSE

Scientists found this mouse at a height of exactly 6,739 m above sea level, where the air is thin. There is less than half the amount of oxygen to breathe up there compared with living at the bottom of the mountain. Snowfields also cover the ground, and the temperature can plunge to minus 14°C. It's not a normal place for a mouse to live, as small animals lose heat rapidly.

MYSTERY MOUSE

The volcano's summit is so remote that the scientists who discovered the mouse had to climb for nearly ten hours to reach the top. They call the little animal the yellow-rumped leaf-eared mouse, and it's a record breaker. It lives at a higher altitude than any other mammal on the planet; in fact, it occurs 2,000 m above the upper limit that green plants can grow, so what, the scientists wonder, is the mouse eating? For now, it remains a mystery.

Peregrine Falcon

The peregrine is the fastest living thing on Earth. When catching its prey, it folds back its wings and plunges in an aerial dive, known as a 'stoop', reaching speeds of over 322 kph.

It's a relatively small bird of prey, a member of the falcon family, but it can knock birds as big as pigeons and ducks out of the sky. It nests in out-of-the-way places on cliffsides, in gorges and steep-sided valleys inland and on sea cliffs at the coast, so its eggs and chicks are safe from foxes and rats.

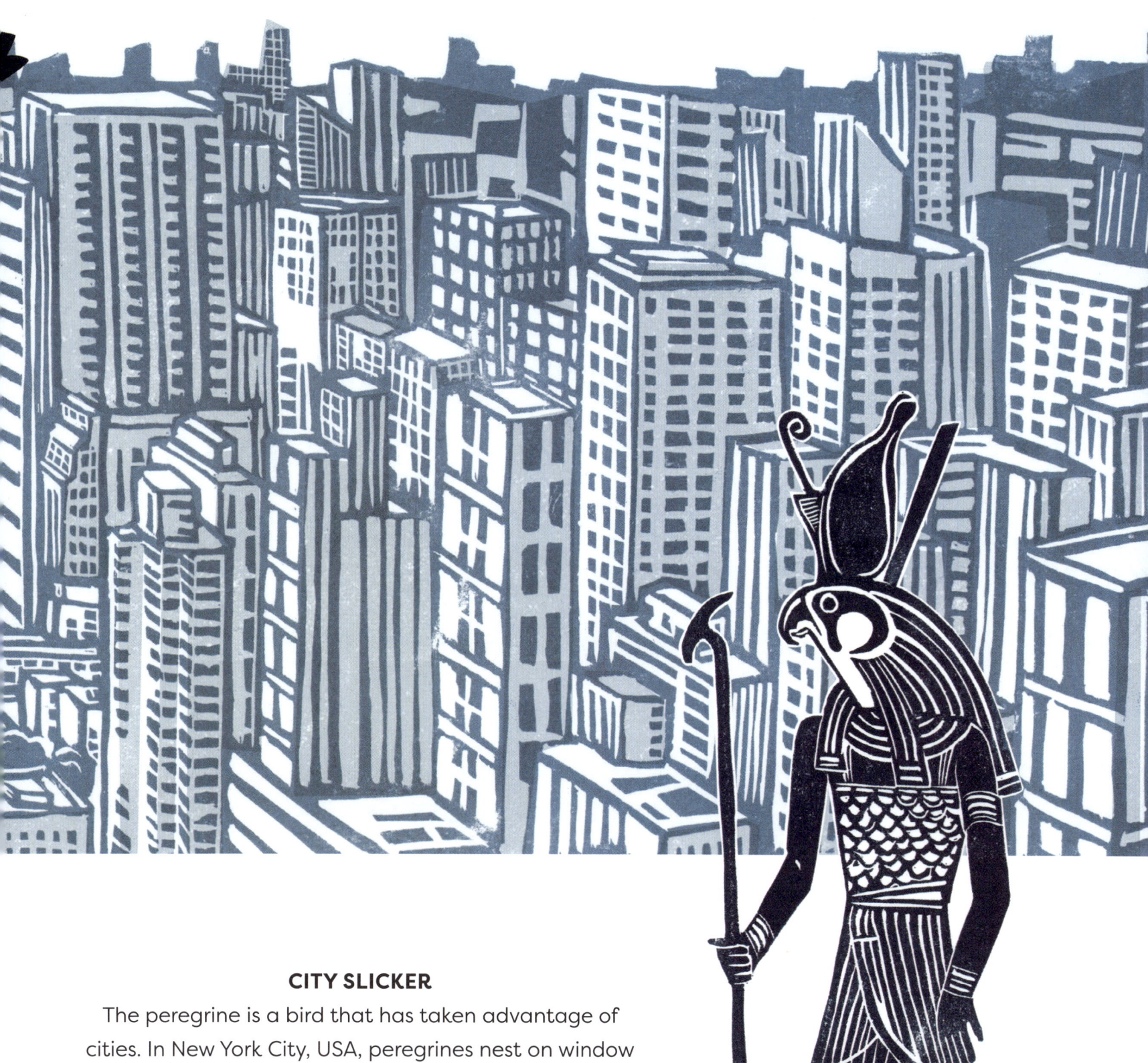

CITY SLICKER

The peregrine is a bird that has taken advantage of cities. In New York City, USA, peregrines nest on window ledges on skyscrapers and hunt feral pigeons along the artificial canyons formed by the high-rise buildings.

The ancient Egyptians worshipped the peregrine. One of their gods (Horus) had a human body with the head of the bird.

Yellow-footed Rock Wallaby

Wallabies live in Australia and on New Guinea, although some have been released into the wild in New Zealand and on the British Isles.

CAMOUFLAGE

Most wallabies have dull brown fur, but the yellow-footed rock wallaby is unusual: it has colourful fur. You would think it would be highly visible, but its stripy patterns help it to blend in with the multi-coloured rocks and cliffs over which it scrambles in the south and east of Australia.

DRY COUNTRY

The wallabies live in small groups in out-of-the-way places, far from humans. They hide from the sun in caves and crevices in the rock during the heat of midday, and come out to feed on grasses and low bushes in late afternoon. They get about by hopping and have a long, striped tail as a balance. They are the only mammals known to transfer water to their babies (known as joeys) by mouth.

Barn Swallow

Throughout the summer in northern Europe, swallows are seen where there are plenty of flying insects – their main food – which they catch on the wing. In the autumn, however, the birds disappear.

The ancient Greek philosopher Aristotle thought they hibernated. In Britain, 18th-century naturalists thought they hibernated underwater, at the bottom of ponds and lakes. It was not until December 1912, when a bird that had been fitted with an identity ring at a nest in Staffordshire, England, was found in Natal, South Africa, that naturalists knew they migrate. They go to Africa for the winter.

SPECIAL SIGNS

When swallows return to Europe to nest, some say 'it is the first sign of spring'. In medieval times farmers were careful not to damage a swallow's nest, for the superstition was that it led to cows producing no milk and hens laying no eggs.

Sailors welcomed the sight of a swallow for they thought it brought them good luck. Being a land bird, land couldn't be far away, and some sailors would have a tattoo of a swallow put on their arm after their first 5,000 nautical miles at sea, and a second tattoo after 10,000. They were symbols of a safe return.

Below

Under the surface of the land and sea are hidden worlds, where plants and animals live their lives away from the prying eyes of humans. People, such as scientists, need special transport and equipment in order to see these living things in their natural home.

CAVE LIFE

Caves can be warm in winter and cool in summer, so many different types of animal visit and rest in caves, away from the cold and the heat. A few live their entire lives in the dark, in great caverns, sometimes many kilometres below the surface.

At dusk, about 20 million Mexican free-tailed bats stream out of Bracken Cave, in Texas, USA, to feed on insects in the surrounding countryside. During the day, they rest deep inside the cave.

BURROWERS AND TUNNELLERS

Burrowing creatures, and even entire plants, also spend their lives under the ground, although at a much shallower depth. A few have even invaded the man-made tunnels that criss-cross our towns and cities.

WATER LIFE

Below the surface of seas, rivers and lakes, animals live at all levels, from those that patrol the surface, where the most food is found, to those that can withstand the enormous pressures in the deepest parts of the ocean. A few make the extraordinary transition from saltwater to freshwater and back again.

The Olm

Cave salamanders live underground in lakes and rivers flowing through some of the deepest cave systems on Earth, so there's little chance of seeing one in its natural home. The European olm is one such cave salamander. It's a ghostly pale pink, eel-shaped amphibian.

BLIND SALAMANDER

As the olm lives permanently in the dark, it has no need to see and is blind. It moves very little, only to catch a passing cave shrimp, and it stores fats and sugars as an insurance policy against times when food is scarce. It can survive for up to 10 years without feeding, if needs be, and can live for 100 years.

HERE BE BABY DRAGONS!

Local people call the olm the 'human fish' on account of its colour, and at one time they thought olms were baby dragons. In North America, cave salamanders, such as the rare Texas blind salamander, are known as 'cave puppets'.

Basking Shark

The world's second largest fish is the basking shark, but it's not dangerous. The 8-m-long giant has an enormous mouth with which it gathers and filters plankton from the sea. In summer months, it often feeds close to shore, where it can be spotted from cliff tops and headlands.

LONG MIGRATION

In winter, it disappears to deeper waters, with some individuals travelling nearly 10,000 km across the Atlantic Ocean from the British Isles to North America. Off the east coast of North America, basking sharks migrate from New England to as far south as the mouth of the Amazon River.

WASHED ASHORE

Dead basking sharks sometimes wash up on beaches, but their tissues rot in such a way as to look like prehistoric marine reptiles. What is often left is the long vertebral column, along with a small head on a longish neck, and with what look like flippers – much like an extinct plesiosaur.

Cave Swiftlets

White-nest swiftlets are small birds in the swift family that live in Southeast Asia. They hunt insects in the rainforest for most of their lives, but, when it's time to nest, they enter caves.

They build their nests in the darkness, on the walls of enormous caverns, some the size of cathedrals, where they are safe from predators. The nests are unusual because they're made totally of spit. The birds build layer upon layer of spit, which dries to form small cup-shaped nests that are 'glued' to the vertical cavern walls.

DANGER AT THE DOOR

When the swiftlet chicks hatch, the parents bring them food from the forest, such as flying insects, but they have to watch out. A type of python, known as a cave racer snake, coils itself around stalactites in narrow passageways and near the cave entrance and grabs birds as they fly in or out.

UNUSUAL SOUP

Early in the breeding season local people collect the nests as they are the main ingredients in birds' nest soup, a delicacy in Chinese cooking. If they take the early nests, the birds build new ones, and breeding is not upset. As so few nests are collected, each is extremely valuable. It makes the swiftlet nest one of the most expensive animal products consumed by people.

The Mole

Moles live their lives almost entirely under the ground. They can survive in tunnels with low oxygen levels because they have special blood that collects more oxygen than most other mammals. They dig constantly in search of earthworms, occasionally pushing up soil to the surface to form molehills, one of the few occasions that we know they exist at all.

ONE OF NATURE'S STARS

North America's star-nosed mole has a rosette of touch-sensitive tentacles on its nose, while other moles have a pointy snout. All have big front feet for digging and an extra 'thumb' next to their regular thumb to make their feet more spade-like. They are not blind or deaf, but their eyes and ears are very small.

WORLD'S FASTEST FEEDER

The North American star-nosed mole can not only swim but also smell underwater. It is the fastest-eating mammal, taking just 120 milliseconds to identify something edible and then eat it.

33

Western Underground Orchid

If a sweet smell comes from a crack in the ground in broom bush country near the town of Corrigin in Western Australia, you might have found a very strange flower. It's an orchid that blooms underground – the western underground orchid.

This orchid has no leaves, but simply consists of a white underground storage stem or tuber that invades the roots of broom honeymyrtle, from which it takes food.

HIDDEN FLOWER

The head of the flower consists of more than 100 tiny maroon flowerlets, but very few people see them. Their fragrance and nectar, on the other hand, attract underground insects, such as termites, which pollinate them. The seeds take as long as six months to mature, but nobody knows how they are distributed around the countryside. A creature must carry them, but no one knows which one.

ABOVE AND BELOW

On the east coast of Australia, the orchid's close relative – the eastern underground orchid – does have flowers that reach the surface, but the western species spends its entire life under the earth.

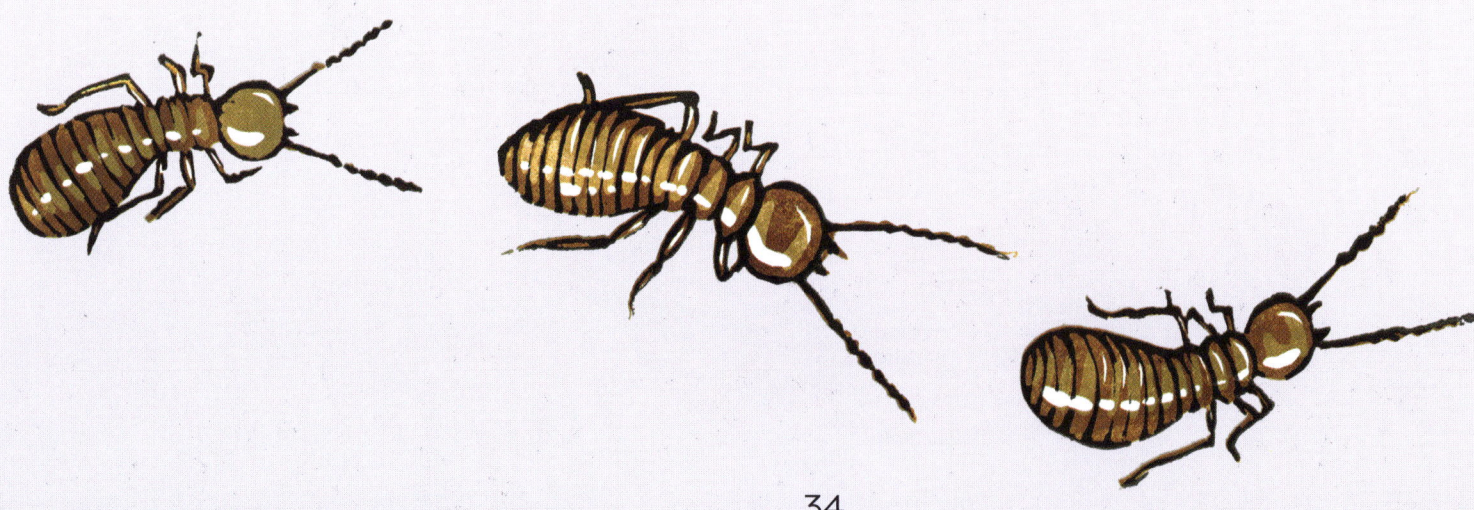

Brown Rat

You very rarely see rats, even though people living in towns and cities are said never to be far from one. In the wild, they prefer damp riverbanks, but it is their fondness for sewage systems and the way they spread diseases that have given them such a bad reputation.

EXPERT SCAVENGERS

Rats will eat almost anything, but when they try a new food they nibble it over a long period. If something tastes odd, like poison bait put down by a rat catcher, they'll avoid it, and they learn from each other what's good or bad.

LEAVING THE SHIP

It's the perception of rats being clever animals that has led to all kinds of superstitions, the most well known being that rats will leave a ship that's likely to sink, even though it appears to be in good repair. The notion comes from a time in 1889, when people working on the American riverboat *Paris C. Brown*, travelling between Louisiana and Ohio, noticed that rats were leaving the ship. They did not reboard the vessel and shortly afterwards, it hit an obstacle in the river and sank.

Common Eel

On both sides of the Atlantic, the snake-like eel has always been a mysterious creature, but its life cycle is now being revealed.

The eel starts life in the Sargasso Sea, in the southwest part of the North Atlantic. Then, as a ribbon-shaped larva, it drifts in the ocean currents towards Europe or North America, depending on the species.

SEA TO RIVER

On reaching the coast the eel larva transforms into a 'glass eel', which, according to medieval folklore, springs from the hair of a horse's tail. The fish then enters an estuary, changes into an 'elver' and heads upstream to a lake, river or stream where it spends most of its life.

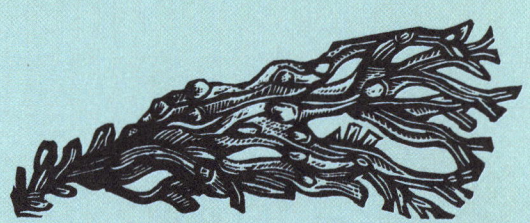

RIVER TO SEA

As the eel grows, it becomes a 'yellow eel' and, after maybe 20 years in fresh water, changes into a 'silver eel' that travels in the opposite direction, sometimes squirming over land to reach a river that goes down to the sea. It then follows the ocean currents back to the Sargasso Sea where eggs are laid and the life cycle starts all over again.

Mariana Snailfish

The fish that lives at the greatest depth of any known fish is the Mariana snailfish. It's pink in colour and has a see-through body, so you can see its vital organs inside. Not much is known about it as its home is so remote.

IN THE DEEPEST DEEP

To observe the snailfish in its natural home, you would need a very special submarine that could resist the crushing pressures at depths down to 8,178 m in the Mariana Trench, the deepest place in the world's oceans. The trench is located in the western Pacific Ocean, but the seabed there is so difficult to reach that only a handful of people have ever been down there.

Long Ago

About 99.9 per cent of plants and animals that ever lived are actually extinct, but they are not all forgotten as the remains of some of them are preserved as fossils.

RECORD OF THE PAST

Fossils can be made of stone or the minerals that replace the animal's dead body, or they can be an impression that the body makes in mud or sand, which, over millions of years, is turned into rock. And, there they remain undisturbed until someone comes along, breaks open the rock and reveals the fossil – maybe a new discovery!

LIVING FOSSILS

There are modern plants and animals that are remarkably similar to those that lived all those millions of years ago, so they are known as 'living fossils'. Their evolution has not stopped during that time. They have changed from their ancient ancestors, but not by very much.

Pterosaurs were ancient flying reptiles that lived between 228 and 66 million years ago. They were the first animals with backbones to evolve powered flight. Some could also climb trees and others could walk on all fours. One was the largest flying animal that ever lived.

43

Ammonite

Ammonites are extinct relatives of the pearly nautilus, squid and octopus. They disappeared at the same time as the dinosaurs, but their fossils can be found in rocks that are between 250 and 65 million years old.

ANCIENT SHELLFISH

Many have a coiled shell, a bit like a snail. When they were alive, they would have had a writhing mass of long, thin tentacle-like arms protruding from the open end of the shell, but those soft parts rarely turn to stone, only the shell. Dolphin-like ichthyosaurs fed on them.

SNAKESTONES

The fossils can be made of stone or a mineral, such as brassy 'fool's gold', and in the northeast of England they are known as 'Whitby snakestones'. Legend has it that there were many snakes living in the vicinity of Whitby and an abbess living there turned them into coils of stone. St Cuthbert of Lindisfarne cursed them and left them headless, although in Victorian times (1837–1901) people carved snakes' heads on the end of the coils, hence the name snakestones.

Megalodon

Imagine a great white shark that's almost twice as long as a London bus, with jaws that could swallow a fully grown person whole, and teeth as big as your hand ...

... and that's megalodon, a colossal shark that fed on whales between twenty and four million years ago. It was one of the largest predators ever to have lived on Earth.

ENORMOUS TEETH

We know megalodon existed because its enormous teeth have been found; but that's about all. Sharks have a skeleton made of cartilage, rather than bone, and cartilage rots away before it can be fossilised, leaving only the teeth.

DRAGON'S TONGUES

In the Mediterranean, ancient Greeks and Romans thought sharks' teeth were the petrified tongues of dragons, and they were supposed to have magical properties. It was said that they could be used to heal snakebites, and, if they were put into wine, they would reveal whether it was poisoned or not.

Jurassic Oyster

The 'devil's toenail', or Gryphaea *as it is known to fossil hunters, is an ancient type of oyster. While dinosaurs were making their presence felt on land, and huge sea-going reptiles – similar in shape to modern dolphins and called ichthyosaurs – dominated the oceans,* Gryphaea *sat in large colonies, partly buried in the mud on the floor of warm shallow seas.*

FILTER FEEDER

Like all oysters, *Gryphaea* had two shells, one large – the claw-like toenail – and the other a smaller, flatter lid. The animal's soft parts were sandwiched between the two. In the same way as modern oysters, this Jurassic oyster filtered out plankton from seawater for food.

OYSTER CURE

This family of oysters lived for many millions of years, but about 34 million years ago they all went extinct. It's thought that a rapid increase in the number of creatures that could crush their shells led to their downfall; but they had a kind of life after death. In medieval times, people carried the fossil shell in their pocket as a cure for rheumatism.

Trilobite

Trilobites appeared in the seas about 520 million years ago. They were distantly related to crustaceans, spiders and insects, and many types were shaped like modern horseshoe crabs, while others resembled woodlice (pillbugs). They were among the first animals to have a front end and a back end, and move forwards.

ALL PARTS OF THE OCEAN

Most trilobites, but not all, had eyes at their front end. Some eyes were quite complex, like the compound eyes of dragonflies. They lived at all levels in the sea, some preferring shallow waters, while others slithered across the deep sea floor. Blind types probably burrowed through mud on the seabed.

FIRST DEFENCE

Trilobite fossils are found in rocks in many parts of the world, but in Canada and Russia, trilobites about 500 million years old have been found rolled up like woodlice to protect themselves from predators. It is the earliest known example of an animal defending itself.

Coelacanth

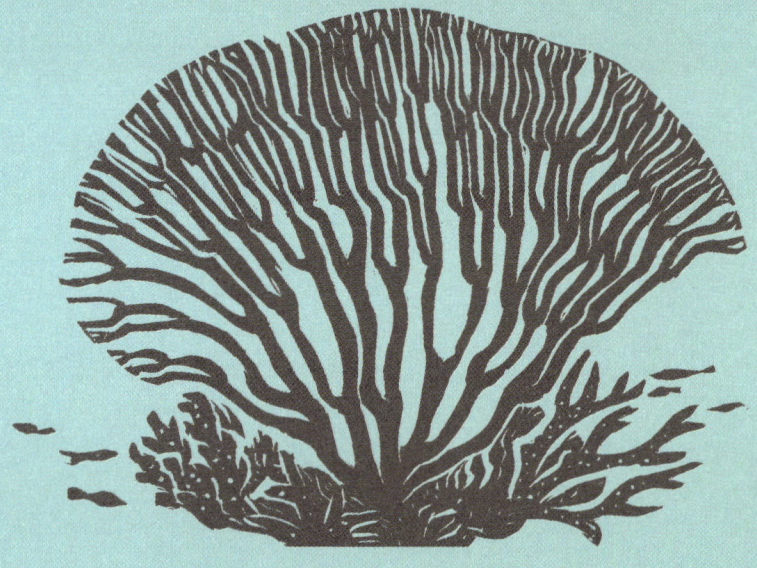

A strange blue-coloured fish, called a coelacanth, is probably the most well known living fossil. Real fossils of its closest relatives are found in rocks about 400 million years old, and the living coelacanth has changed very little in all that time.

OLD FOUR-LEGS

The coelacanth's lobe-shaped fins resemble legs, and, indeed, coelacanths are related to the ancient fish that eventually developed legs and emerged from the water to conquer the land. It was thought that the family had become extinct, along with the dinosaurs, but in 1938 an individual was caught by a South African fishing boat and nicknamed 'Old Four-legs'.

MODERN COELACANTHS

Today, scientists know of two populations of coelacanths. One population lives in the sea between Africa and Madagascar, in the western Indian Ocean, where the fish rest during the day in deep underwater caves. Another population can be found off the coast of Sulawesi in the eastern Indian Ocean.

Horseshoe Crab

First appearing about 450 million years ago, horseshoe crabs are included as living fossils, but they are not crabs; they're more closely related to spiders.

They are shaped like trilobites, so they certainly look primitive. Their body is protected by a hard covering or carapace, and underneath are several sets of jointed legs, some used for walking and others for holding food.

BEACH INVASION

Horseshoe crabs live on the seabed in coastal waters, but emerge from the sea to lay their eggs in the sand on beaches. It's the only time you are likely to see one alive in the wild. In some places, such as Delaware Bay, on the east coast of North America, thousands crawl out of the sea at the same time. Migrating birds feed on the eggs, timing their own arrival to coincide with the mass emergence of the horseshoe crabs. The extraordinary event is like a scene from a time long ago.

The Gingko

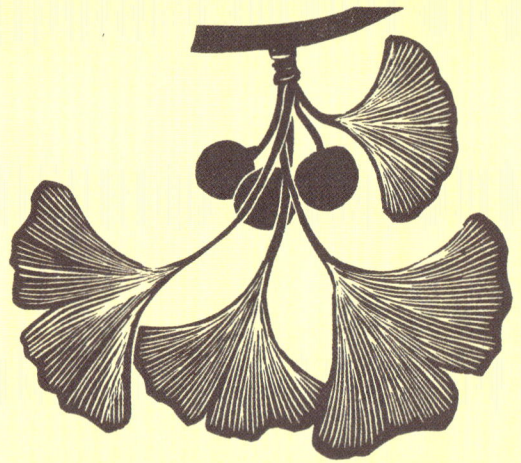

The ginkgo tree is a living fossil. Its fossil remains have been found in rocks over 200 million years old, which means it was growing when the dinosaurs were prowling Earth.

NEIGHBOURHOOD TREE

Today, the ginkgo is found growing in the wild only in China, but, because it is such an attractive tree, it has been cultivated all over the world and is often found in parks, streets and gardens, so there might be one growing near you.

YELLOW IN AUTUMN

Its delicate fan-shaped leaves are similar to the fronds of the maidenhair fern, so the tree is sometimes called the 'maidenhair tree'. In its natural home, it can grow to be 50 m tall, and its branches can be all higgledy-piggledy, with long and short branches growing at right angles. In the autumn, ginkgo leaves turn bright yellow.

NATURAL MEDICINE

In China, ginkgo is an ingredient in traditional medicine and ginkgo extract can be found for sale in health food shops around the world.

Tuatara

New Zealand's tuatara looks like a lizard but it isn't one. It's related to a group of lizard-like reptiles that had their heyday 200 million years ago, and the tuatara is the only survivor, so it is a living fossil.

THREE EYES

Its most interesting feature is its 'third eye' in the top of its head. It's only visible in young tuatara, for it becomes covered in dark scales as they get older. It is thought that it could have several functions: to detect when it's night and day, for example, and to help the reptile be in the right place to get warm or to cool down.

SURVIVORS

Unlike most reptiles, tuatara can remain active at unusually low temperatures – as low as 5°C – but high temperatures – above 28°C – can kill them. Introduced rats also kill them, and tuatara nearly went extinct like their ancient relatives, but they have been saved in the nick of time.

DARK MESSENGER

The reptile features in Māori (the Indigenous people of New Zealand) legends, in which the reptiles are said to be the messengers of the lord of darkness and all that is evil.

Where in the World?

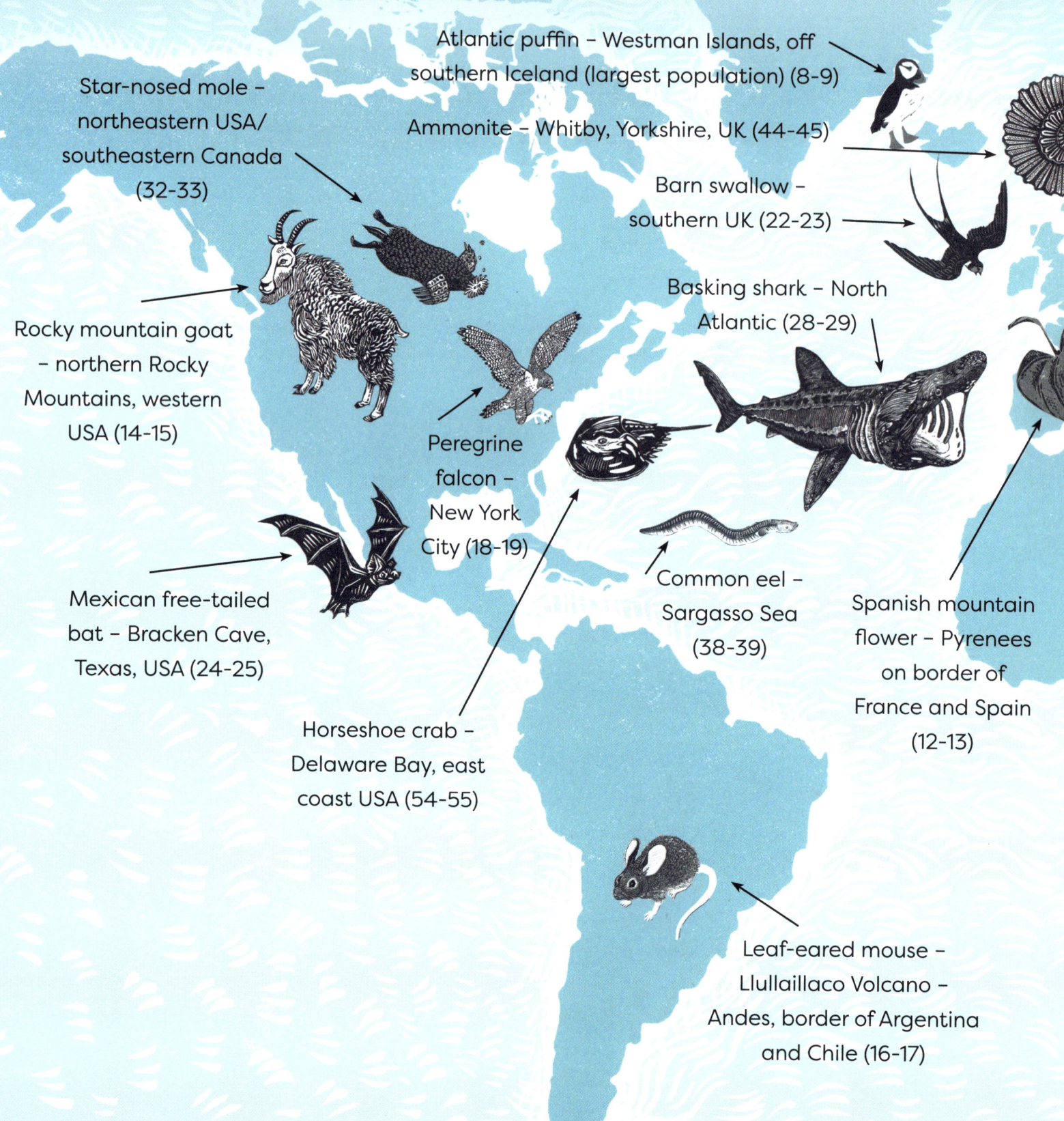

Star-nosed mole – northeastern USA/ southeastern Canada (32-33)

Atlantic puffin – Westman Islands, off southern Iceland (largest population) (8-9)

Ammonite – Whitby, Yorkshire, UK (44-45)

Barn swallow – southern UK (22-23)

Rocky mountain goat – northern Rocky Mountains, western USA (14-15)

Basking shark – North Atlantic (28-29)

Peregrine falcon – New York City (18-19)

Mexican free-tailed bat – Bracken Cave, Texas, USA (24-25)

Common eel – Sargasso Sea (38-39)

Spanish mountain flower – Pyrenees on border of France and Spain (12-13)

Horseshoe crab – Delaware Bay, east coast USA (54-55)

Leaf-eared mouse – Llullaillaco Volcano – Andes, border of Argentina and Chile (16-17)

Some of the plants and animals we have been reading about are found almost everywhere in the world, like the brown rat, which may be hidden away, but lives on every continent except Antarctica. Others you can only see in very particular places, such as the Spanish mountain flower on a single crag in Spain and the leaf-eared mouse that lives on its own volcano in South America. A few, like the peregrine falcon, have forsaken their natural home and taken advantage of what's on offer in cities. Let's see where the others might be found.

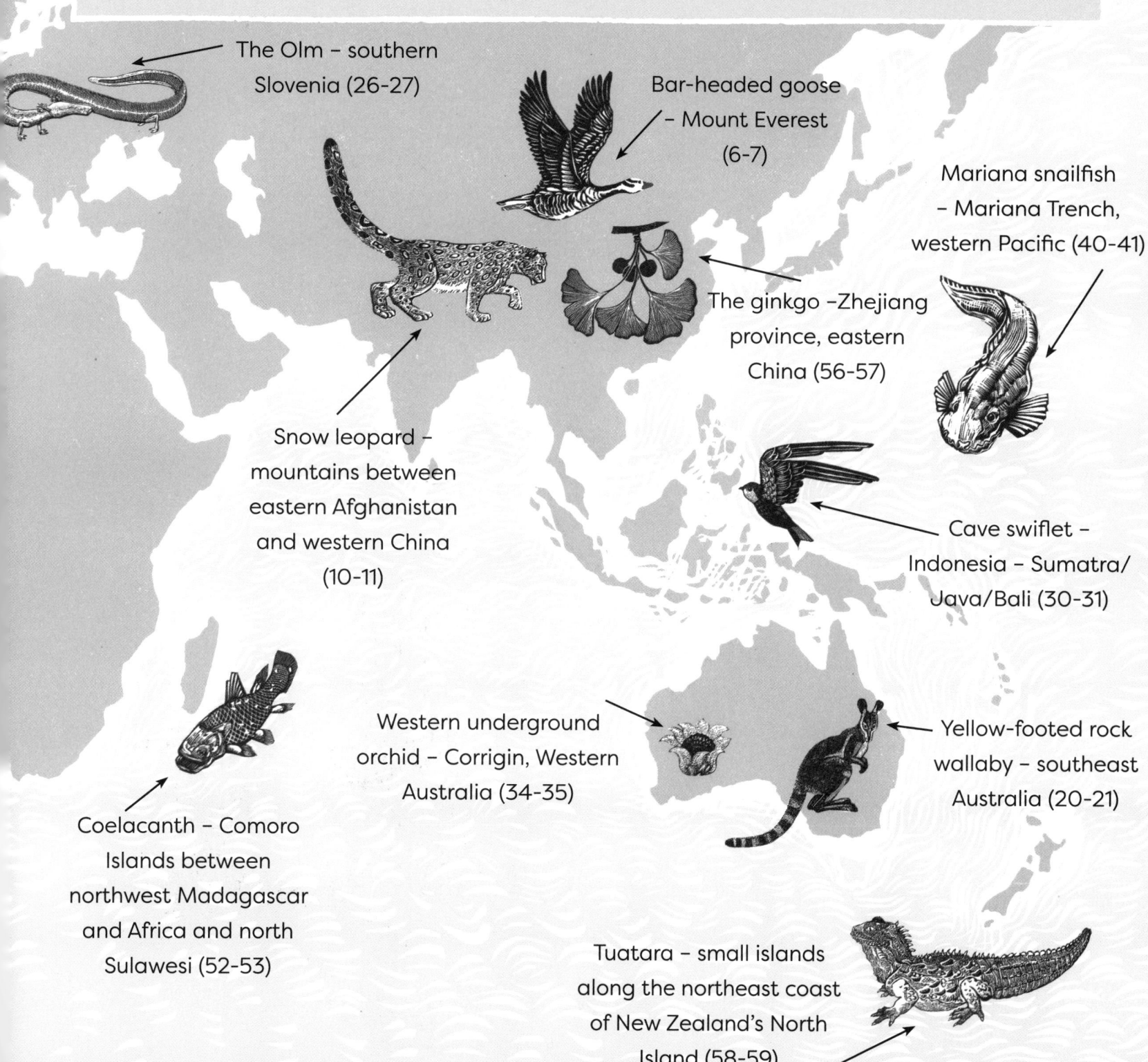

The Olm – southern Slovenia (26-27)

Bar-headed goose – Mount Everest (6-7)

Mariana snailfish – Mariana Trench, western Pacific (40-41)

The ginkgo –Zhejiang province, eastern China (56-57)

Snow leopard – mountains between eastern Afghanistan and western China (10-11)

Cave swiflet – Indonesia – Sumatra/ Java/Bali (30-31)

Coelacanth – Comoro Islands between northwest Madagascar and Africa and north Sulawesi (52-53)

Western underground orchid – Corrigin, Western Australia (34-35)

Yellow-footed rock wallaby – southeast Australia (20-21)

Tuatara – small islands along the northeast coast of New Zealand's North Island (58-59)

Glossary

accommodate	to fit in with the needs of something
adapted	the process by which a species becomes fitted to its environment
amphibian	animal with a backbone that lives both on land and in water
bird of prey	a bird with a hooked bill and sharp talons that feeds on other animals
cartilage	bendy material like that in your nose and outer ear
cloven hoof	hoof or foot with a split in it
compound eye	eye with lots of tiny lenses
delicacy	something that's nice to eat
estuary	part of a river that enters the sea
evolution	the theory that all the kinds of living thing that exist today developed from earlier types over many years
extinct	when a type of animal dies out and has gone forever
feral	a pet or farm animal that lives in the wild
folklore	ancient stories that people told about their lives
gorge	a narrow steep-walled canyon or part of a canyon
hibernate	to hide away and be inactive or sleep through cold spells
larva	young stage in an animal's life between egg and adult
limestone	rock made of the bodies of microscopic living things
mammal	animal with backbone and hair that feeds its young milk
medieval	a period in history from 1100 to 1500 CE
migration	when animals move from one region to another as the seasons change
mountaineer	someone who climbs mountains
multitasking	to be able to do lots of different things at the same time
naturalist	an expert in natural history (the study of plants and animals)
nautical mile	the unit of length used in sea and air navigation, equal to 1,853 m

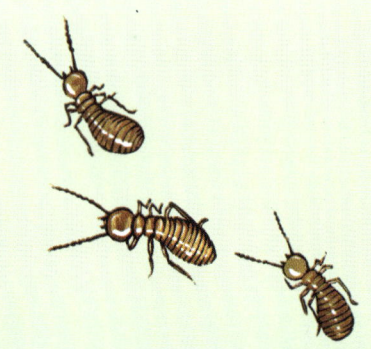

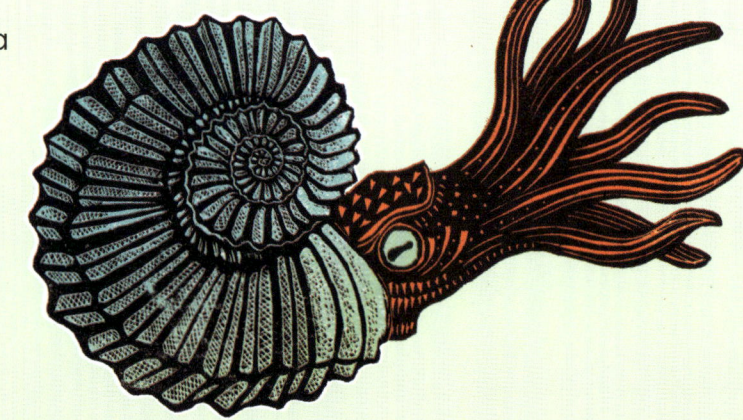

nectar	sweet substance produced by flowers
ocean current	the movement of seawater caused by forces such as the wind
petrified	turned to stone
philosopher	somebody who thinks deeply about the world and life
plankton	animals and plant-like living things that float about in the sea
pollinate	to take pollen from one flower to another
predator	animal that hunts and eats other animals
primitive	ancient and simpler features rather than modern ones
reptile	animal with a backbone and covered with scales
sheer	very steep, almost vertical
skyscraper	very tall building
species	types of plant and animal
stalactite	a structure, made from minerals, which hangs from the ceiling of caves
summit	the top of a mountain
superstition	belief that things are lucky or unlucky
tentacles	long, thin parts of an animal for holding or feeling things
transition	when something changes from one thing to another
vertebral column	backbone

How the illustrations are made

My printmaking process starts with drawing – usually in pencil. Once I'm happy with my design, I trace it onto a linoleum (lino) block. I separate the different coloured parts of the drawing into layers, from light to dark. Using cutting tools, I start by carving away the bits of lino I don't want to print; these areas will show the white of the paper. Using a roller, I ink up the lino and position the paper using registration lines, and then apply pressure to the paper/lino, either with a printing press or by hand with a baren or spoon. This process is repeated on the same lino block working on the next darkest colour layer; this is called a reduction print. I carve a separate block for the darkest layer with the most detail; this is called a key block. Usually, I print the layers onto separate pieces of paper, but sometimes – if there's enough drying time – I'll make a single print. Finally, I scan the prints into the computer, assembling the layers to compose the complete illustration.

Index

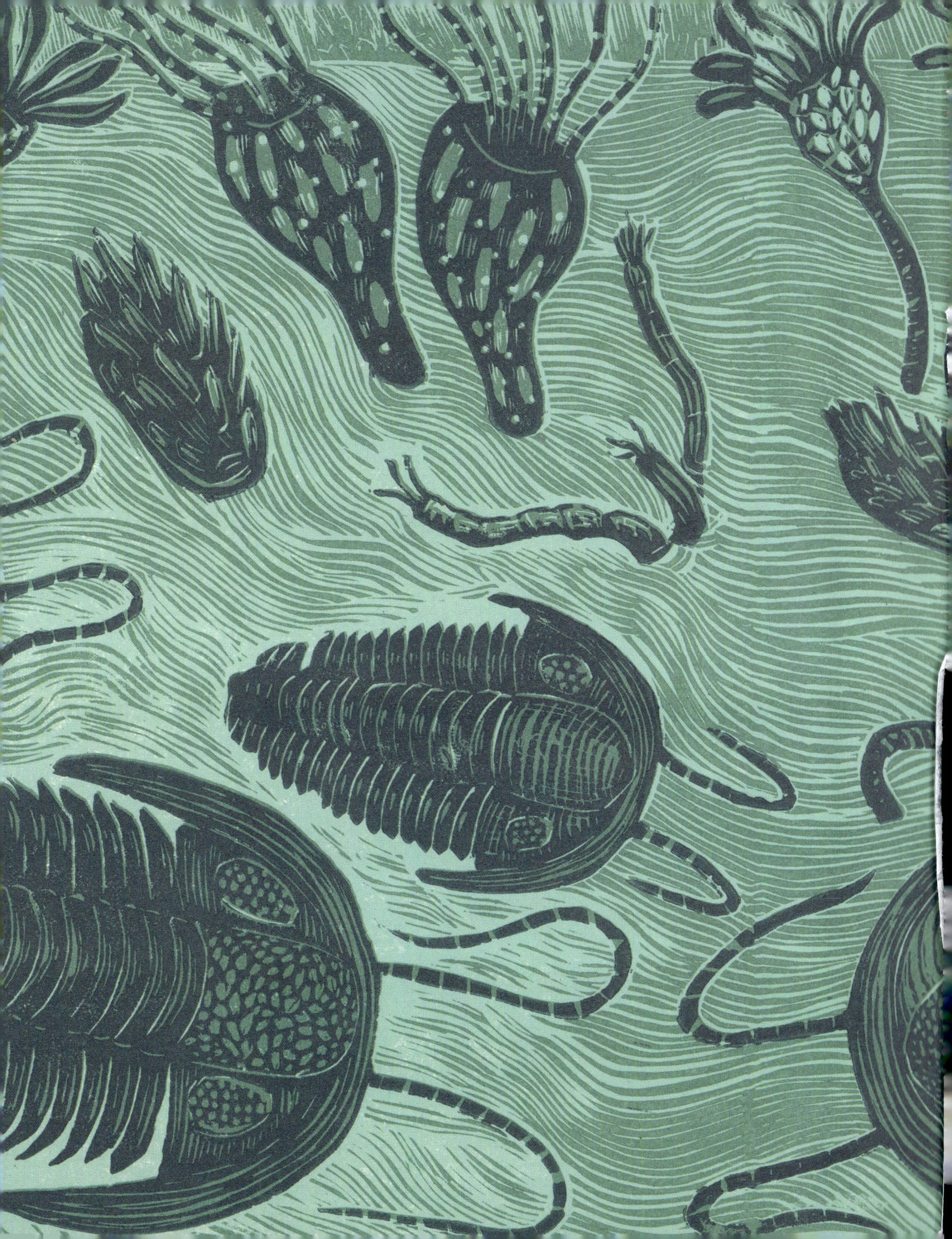